World Capitals

150 Questions and Answers

James Magee

Other books by this author can be found at
www.littrivia.com

Copyright registered in 2013 by James J. Magee. All rights are reserved. Unless permitted by U.S. Copyright Law, no part of this book may be produced in any form, including information storage and retrieval systems without permission in writing from the publisher. First paperback printing was in 2013.

The aim of this book . . .

There are 150 questions and answers about countries and their respective capitals. While the multiple choice questions focus on the world's capitals, every fifteenth question will examine some geographical quirk that occurs geographically. An Index at the end of the book will list every country (its capital) and the page that it is on which will have exact directions on how to locate it on a globe or atlas.

Along with the capitals provided in the answer will be the bordering countries of the country in question. It is suggested that the reader have an atlas or globe available to trace these boundaries and familiarize themselves with the location of the country being discussed. [Hint: The two incorrect capitals given in the selection will be in the same area of the globe as the correct capital or even in the same country].

Some capitals that most people already know will be omitted. For instance, England (London), France (Paris), Germany (Berlin), Ireland (Dublin), Northern Ireland (Belfast), Italy (Rome), Greece (Athens), , China (Beijing), Russia (), U.S.A. Washington, D.C. etc.

<u>World Capitals</u> can be found on <u>www.littrivia.com</u> along with other books by this author.

QUESTION # 1

What is the South American capital of Bolivia? Is it a) La Paz and Sucre b) Santiago or c) Santa Cruz de la Sierra?

QUESTION # 2

What is the capital of Sudan? Is it a) Abuja b) Khartoum or c) N'Djamena?

ANSWER # 1

The two capitals of Bolivia are La Paz and Sucre. Bolivia is landlocked and is bordered by Brazil to the north and east; Paraguay and Argentina to the south; Chile to the southwest and Peru to the west. While Sucre is the judicial capital, La Paz is the administrative capital.

ANSWER # 2

The capital of Sudan is Khartoum. Sudan is bordered by Egypt to the north; the Red Sea to the northeast; Ethiopia and Eritrea to the east; South Sudan to the south; Central African Republic to the southwest; Chad to the west and Libya to the northwest.

QUESTION # 3

What is the capital of Afghanistan? Is it a) New Delhi b) Islamabad or c) Kabul?

QUESTION # 4

What is the capital of Hungary? Is it a) Budapest b) Prague or c) Warsaw?

ANSWER # 3

The capital of Afghanistan is Kabul. The Republic of Afghanistan borders five countries on the continent of Asia: Iran to the west: Turkmenistan to the north-west, Uzbekistan to the north, Tajikistan to the north-east and Pakistan to the east and south.

ANSWER # 4

The capital of Hungary is Budapest. Hungary is bordered by eight countries: Slovakia on the north, Ukraine on the north east, Romanic on the south east, Serbia and Montenegro on the south, Croatia on the south west, Slovenia on the west, and Austria on the north west.

QUESTION # 5

What is the capital of New Zealand? Is it a) Auckland b) Wellington or c) Christchurch?

QUESTION # 6

What is the capital of Japan? Is it a) Taipei b) Seoul or c) Tokyo?

ANSWER # 5

The capital of New Zealand is Wellington. New Zealand is an island country in the southwestern Pacific Ocean. It is situated some 900 miles east of Australia across the Tasman Sea and 600 miles south of New Caledonia, Fiji and Tonga.

ANSWER # 6

The capital of Japan is Tokyo. Japan is an island nation of East Asia. It is southeast of the Russian Far East, separated by the Sea of Okhotsk;; slightly east of Korea, separated by the Sea of Japan; east-northeast of China and Taiwan, separated by the East China Sea.

QUESTION # 7

What is the capital of Uruguay? Is it a) Montevideo b) Caracas or c) Buenos Aires?

QUESTION # 8

What is the capital of Uganda? Is it a) Kinshasa b) Kampala or c) Libreville?

ANSWER # 7

The capital of Uruguay is Montevideo. Uruguay is located between Argentina and Brazil, from which it became independent from in 1825. Its grasslands provide good grazing for cattle and sheep, making hides and wool two of Uruguay's most important exports.

ANSWER # 8

The capital of Uganda is Kampala. Uganda is a landlocked country in South Africa. It is bordered on the east by Kenya; on the north by South Sudan; on the west by the Democratic Republic of the Congo; on the southwest by Rwanda and on the south by Tanzania.

QUESTION # 9

What is the capital of Ukraine? Is it a) Tbilisi b) Astana or c) Kiev?

QUESTION # 10

What is the capital of Australia? Is it a) Canberra b) Sidney or c) Melbourne?

ANSWER # 9

The capital of Ukraine is Kiev. Ukraine borders the Russian Federation to the east and northeast; Belarus to the northwest; Poland, Slovakia and Hungary to the west; Romania and Moldova to the southwest and the Black Sea and the Sea of Azov to the south and southeast.

ANSWER # 10

The capital of Australia is Canberra. Neighboring countries include Indonesia, East Timor and Papua New Guinea to the north; Solomon Islands, Vanuatu and New Caledonia to the northeast; and New Zealand to the southeast. It includes the island of Tasmania and smaller islands.

QUESTION # 11

What is the capital of Iceland? Is it a) Oslo b) Reykjavik or c) Copenhagen?

QUESTION # 12

What is the capital of Barbados? Is it a) Saint George's b) Saint John's or c) Bridgetown?

ANSWER # 11

The capital of Iceland is Reykjavik. Iceland is a Nordic European island country situated at the confluence of the North Atlantic and Arctic Oceans, on the Mid-Atlantic Ridge. It is referred to as "the land of the midnight sun" due to the tilt of earth's axis during the summer.

ANSWER # 12

The capital of Barbados is Bridgetown. Barbados is an island country in the Lesser Antilles. It is situated in the western area of the North Atlantic and 62 miles east of the Windward Islands and the Caribbean Sea. It is 104 miles east of the island of Saint Vincent.

QUESTION # 13

What is the capital of Columbia? Is it a) Bogota b) Caracas or c) La Paz?

QUESTION # 14

What is the capital of Somalia? Is it a) Nairobi b) Mogadishu or c) Dakar?

ANSWER # 13

> The capital of Columbia is Bogota. Columbia is bordered to the east by Venezuela and Brazil; to the south by Ecuador and Peru; to the north by the Caribbean Sea; and to the northwest by Panama. Columbia's main river is the Magdalena River.

ANSWER # 14

> The capital of Somalia is Mogadishu. Located at the Horn of Africa (peninsula that juts into the Arabian Sea), Somalia is bordered by Ethiopia to the west; Djibouti to the northwest; the Gulf of Aden to the north; the Indian Ocean to the east and Kenya to the southwest.

QUESTION # 15

What are the Tropics and where are they located?

QUESTION # 16

What is the capital of Turkey? Is it a) Ankara b) Zagreb or c) Yerevan?

ANSWER # 15

The Tropics is a region of the Earth surrounding the Equator. It is limited in latitude by the Tropic of Cancer in the northern hemisphere and the Tropic of Capricorn in the southern hemisphere. These latitudes correspond to the axial tilt of the Earth.

ANSWER # 16

The capital of Turkey is Ankara. Turkey is bordered by eight countries: Bulgaria to the northwest; Greece to the west; Georgia to the northeast; Armenia, Iran and the Azerbaijani enclave of Nakhchivan to the east and Iraq and to the southeast.

QUESTION # 17

What is the capital of Austria? Is it a) Budapest b) Vienna or c) Bucharest?

QUESTION # 18

What is the capital of Jamaica? Is it a) Managua b) Belmopan or c) Kingston?

ANSWER # 17

The capital of Austria is Vienna. Austria is bordered by the Czech Republic and Germany to the north; Hungary and Slovakia to the east; Slovenia and Italy to the south; and Switzerland and Liechtenstein to the west. The Danube River flows through Austria.

ANSWER # 18

The capital of Jamaica is Kingston. Jamaica is an island nation of the Greater Antilles, located in the northwestern Caribbean Sea, south of Cuba and west of the island of Hispaniola where Haiti and the Dominican Republic are located. Jamaica is approximately 146 miles long.

QUESTION # 19

What is the South American capital of Paraguay? Is it a) Asuncion b) Quito or c) Bogota?

QUESTION # 20

What is the capital of Libya? Is it a) Nairobi b) Tripoli or c) Addis Ababa?

ANSWER # 19

The capital of Paraguay is Asuncion. Paraguay is bordered by Argentina to the south and southwest; Brazil to the east and northeast and Bolivia to the northwest. Paraguay is landlocked and the Paraguay River runs north to south through the center of the country.

ANSWER # 20

The capital of Libya is Tripoli. Libya lies in the Maghreb region of North Africa. This country is bordered by the Mediterranean Sea to the north; Egypt to the east; Sudan to the southeast; Chad and Niger to the south and Algeria and Tunis to the west.

QUESTION # 21

What is the capital of Bulgaria? Is it a) Tirana b) Bucharest or c) Sofia?

QUESTION # 22

What is the capital of The Netherlands? Is it a) Amsterdam b) Brussels or c) Bern?

ANSWER # 21

The capital of Bulgaria is Sofia. This Southeastern European country is bordered by Romania to the north; Serbia and Macedonia to the west; Greece and Turkey to the south and the Black Sea to the east. Bulgaria occupies a portion of the eastern Balkan Peninsula.

ANSWER # 22

The capital of The Netherlands is Amsterdam. The Netherlands is located in Western Europe at the mouth of three major rivers: the Rhine River, the Maas River and the Scheldt River. Belgium and Germany are the two countries that are its borders. On the west is the North Sea.

QUESTION # 23

What is the capital of Nicaragua? Is it a) Kingston b) Managua or c) Belmopan?

QUESTION # 24

What is the capital of Zambia? Is it a) Bamako b) Yaoundé or c) Lusaka?

ANSWER # 23

The capital of Nicaragua is Managua. This largest Central American country borders Honduras (north) and Costa Rica (south). Mountainous in the west, with fertile valleys, the Pacific coast is volcanic and very fertile. The Caribbean coast is aptly called the "Mosquito Coast."

ANSWER # 24

The capital of Zambia is Lusaka. Seven countries border Zambia: Tanzania and the Democratic Republic of the Congo to the north; Angola to the east; Namibia and Zimbabwe to the south; and Malawi and Mozambique to the east.

QUESTION # 25

What is the capital of Belize? Is it a) Belmopan b) Georgetown or c) Tegucigalpa?

QUESTION # 26

What is the capital of Sweden? Is it a) Oslo b) Stockholm or c) Helsinki?

ANSWER # 25

The capital of Belize is Belmopan. Belize borders the Caribbean Sea along the eastern shore of Central America just below the Yucatan Peninsula. It is bounded on the north and west by Mexico and on the south and west by Guatemala.

ANSWER # 26

The capital of Sweden is Stockholm. Sweden borders on Norway in the west and on Finland in the northeast, on the Gulf of Bothnia in the east, and on the Baltic Sea in the south. In Europe, it occupies the eastern part of the Scandinavian Peninsula.

QUESTION # 27

What is the capital of Guyana? Is it a) Bridgetown b) Paramaribo or c) Georgetown?

QUESTION # 28

What is the capital of The Bahamas? Is it a) Nassau b) Port-au-Prince or c) San Jose?

ANSWER # 27

The capital of Guyana is Georgetown. Guyana is bordered on the north by the Atlantic Ocean; on the east by Suriname; on the south by and west by Brazil; and on the west by Venezuela. Bauxite, gold, diamonds and manganese are mined in Guyana.

ANSWER # 28

The capital of The Bahamas is Nassau. The Commonwealth of the Bahamas is an island group off the eastern coast of Florida in the North Atlantic Ocean. Technically, the island chain is too far north to be considered part of the Caribbean Sea.

QUESTION # 29

What is the capital of Sierra Leone? Is it a) Yamoussoukro b) Freetown or c) Praia?

QUESTION # 30

What is the difference between an Isthmus and a Peninsula?

ANSWER # 29

The capital of Sierra Leone is Freetown. Sierra Leone is bordered by the Atlantic Ocean on the west, by Guinea on the north and west and by Liberia in the south. The name of the capital reflects the country's history as a refuge for freed slaves.

ANSWER # 30

An isthmus is a narrow body of land surrounded by water that connects two larger bodies of land. Panama is an example of an isthmus. A peninsula is a body of land surrounded by water on three sides. Florida is an example of a peninsula (Georgia, Alabama, etc.).

QUESTION # 31

What is the capital of Lithuania? Is it a) Riga b) Tallinn or c) Vilnius?

QUESTION # 32

What is the capital of Serbia? Is it a) Belgrade b) Sofia or c) Tirana?

ANSWER # 31

The capital of Lithuania is Vilnius. Lithuania is bordered by Belarus to the southeast; Baltic-Russia (Kaliningrad) to the southwest; Latvia to the north; Poland to the south and the Baltic Sea to the west. It is one of the three Baltic countries along with Estonia and Latvia.

ANSWER # 32

The capital of Serbia is Belgrade. Serbia is bordered by Hungary to the north; Romania and Bulgaria to the east; Macedonia to the south and Croatia, Bosnia and Montenegro to the west; also it borders Albania through the disputed region of Kosovo.

QUESTION # 33

What is the capital of Costa Rica? Is it a) San Salvador b) San Jose or c) Santa Domingo?

QUESTION # 34

What is the capital of Suriname? Is it a) Tunis b) Abuja or c) Paramaribo?

ANSWER # 33

The capital of Costa Rica is San Jose. This Central American country is bordered by Nicaragua to the north, Panama to the south, the Pacific Ocean to the west and south and the Caribbean Sea to the east. Costa Rica is officially known as the Republic of Costa Rica.

ANSWER # 34

The capital of Suriname is Paramaribo. Suriname is bordered on the west by Guyana; on the south by Brazil; on the east by French Guinea; and on the north by the Atlantic Ocean. [The Dutch traded New York City to the British for the colony of Suriname].

QUESTION # 35

What is the capital of Guinea? Is it a) Conakry b) Bamako or c) Banjul?

QUESTION # 36

What is the capital of Republic of Croatia ? Is it a) Tirana b) Zagreb or c) Sofia?

ANSWER # 35

The capital of Guinea is Conakry. The country of Guinea is bordered by: Cote d'Ivoire, Guinea-Bissau, Liberia, Mali, Senegal and Sierra Leone. Guinea's shape resembles a crescent with its Atlantic coast forming one end. Its other borders form the rest of the crescent.

ANSWER # 36

The capital of Croatia is Zagreb. Boarding countries are: Serbia, Slovenia, Bosnia-Herzegovina, Hungary, and Montenegro. Old Yugoslavia is now six republics: Bosnia-Herzegovina, Croatia, Macedonia, Montenegro, Slovenia and Serbia.

QUESTION # 37

What is the capital of Indonesia? Is it a) Kuala Lumpur b) Bangkok or c) Jakarta?

QUESTION # 38

What is the capital of Chad? Is it a) N'Djamena b) Accra or c) Niamey?

ANSWER # 37

The capital of Indonesia is Jakarta. Indonesia is bordered by Papua New Guinea, East Timor and Malaysia. Indonesia has approximately 17,500 islands [Two Islands - Java and Sumatra].. Before its independence, Indonesia was known as the Dutch East Indies.

ANSWER # 38

The capital of Chad is N'Djamena. The country of Chad is bordered by the Central African Republic on the south, Sudan on the east, Libya on the north with Cameroon, Niger and Nigeria on the west. Northern Chad is part of the Sahara Desert.

QUESTION # 39

What is the capital of Latvia? Is it a) Vilnius b) Riga or c) Tallinn?

QUESTION # 40

What is the capital of Norway? Is it a) Stockholm b) Helsinki or c) Oslo?

ANSWER # 39

The capital of Latvia is Riga. Latvia is bordered to the north by Estonia, to the south by Lithuania, to the east by the Russian Federation and southeast by Belarus. Latvia is one of the three Baltic countries along with Estonia and Lithuania.

ANSWER # 40

The capital of Norway is Oslo. Norway has the longest border with Sweden on its east side. On its northeast it has Finland and Russia. On its west side, it has the North Sea and the Norwegian Sea. In Europe, it occupies the western part of the Scandinavian Peninsula.

QUESTION # 41

What is the capital of Malaysia? Is it a) Kuala Lumpur b) Bangkok or c) Jakarta?

QUESTION # 42

What is the capital of Haiti? Is it a) San Jose b) Port-au-Prince or c) San Juan?

ANSWER # 41

The capital of Malaysia is Kuala Lumpur. The borders of Malaysia include land and maritime borders with Brunei, Indonesia and Thailand and shared maritime boundaries with the Philippines, Singapore and Vietnam.

ANSWER # 42

The capital of Haiti is Port-au-Prince. The Dominican Republic is the only other country on the same island known as Hispaniola. Across the ocean to the northwest is Cuba and across the ocean to the southwest is Jamaica. Haiti is about 750 miles southeast of Florida.

QUESTION # 43

What is the capital of Liberia? Is it a) Lome b) Rabat or c) Monrovia?

QUESTION # 44

What is the capital of Slovenia? Is it a) Ljubljana b) Prague or c) Bucharest?

ANSWER # 43

> The capital of Liberia is Monrovia. Liberia is bordered in the northwest by Sierra Leone, in the northeast by Guinea, in the east by Cote D'Ivoire (Ivory Coast) and in the west by the Atlantic Ocean. The capital, Monrovia, was named after the American president James Monroe.

ANSWER # 44

> The capital of Slovenia is Ljubljana. Slovenia is bordered in the north by Austria, in the northeast by Hungary, in the southeast by Croatia and in the west by Italy. It is located between the southeastern reaches of the Alps and the Adriatic Sea.

QUESTION # 45

Why is Madagascar referred to as a micro-continent when it is just an island (like Greenland) off the coast of Africa?

QUESTION # 46

What is the capital of Honduras? Is it a) San Jose b) Tegucigalpa or c) San Juan?

ANSWER # 45

Madagascar is considered a micro-continent because of its small size and because it lies on a section of continental crust that rifted and drifted apart from the main continental landmass of Africa. [Madagascar has also been referred to as "the eighth continent"].

ANSWER # 46

The capital of Honduras is Tegucigalpa. This triangular-shaped country, which is the second largest Central American republic, is bordered by Guatemala to the west, Nicaragua to the southeast and El Salvador to the southwest. It borders the Caribbean Sea and North Pacific Ocean.

QUESTION # 47

What is the capital of Mali? Is it a) Freetown b) Monrovia or c) Bamako?

QUESTION # 48

What is the capital of Azerbaijan? Is it a) Baku b) Tbilisi or c) Tashkent?

ANSWER # 47

The capital of Mali is Bamako. This landlocked West African country is bordered by Algeria to the north, Niger to the east, Burkina Faso and Cote D'Ivoire to the south, Guinea to the southwest and Senegal and Mauritania to the west.

ANSWER # 48

The capital of Azerbaijan is Baku. Located in the region of the southern Caucus Mountains, this Eurasian country [the size of Portugal] borders the Caspian Sea to the east, Georgia and Russia to the north, Iran to the south and Armenia to south and southwest.

QUESTION # 49

What is the capital of Romania? Is it a) Tirana b) Bucharest or c) Sofia?

QUESTION # 50

What is the capital of Puerto Rico? Is it a) Port-au-Prince b) San Juan or c) Santa Domingo?

ANSWER # 49

The capital of Romania is Bucharest. Located in the Balkan region which borders the Black Sea, Romania shares a border with Hungary and Serbia to the west, Ukraine and Moldova to the northeast and east and Bulgaria to the south.

ANSWER # 50

The capital of Puerto Rico is San Juan. As an island, Puerto Rico does not share any land borders with other countries. The Dominican Republic is 90 miles west and the U.S. Virgin Islands, which border the British Virgin Islands, are about 50 miles to the east.

QUESTION # 51

What is the capital of Egypt? Is it a) Cairo b) Tunis or c) Tripoli?

QUESTION # 52

What is the capital of Belarus? Is it a) Kiev b) Minsk or c) Vilnius?

ANSWER # 51

The capital of Egypt is Cairo. Egypt is located in northeastern Africa is bordered by the following countries: Israel on the east; Libya in the west and Sudan in the south. Egypt controls the Suez Canal which is on its eastern border between the Mediterranean Sea and the Red Sea.

ANSWER # 52

The capital of Belarus is Minsk. Belarus, which is officially known as the Republic of Belarus, is bordered as follow: Latvia and Lithuania (two of the Baltic States, Estonia is the third) to the north, Russia to the east, Ukraine to the south and Poland to the west.

QUESTION # 53

What is the capital of Ecuador? Is it a) La Paz b) Quito or c) Sucre?

QUESTION # 54

What is the capital of Miramar? Is it a) Rangoon b) Vientiane or c) Phnom-Penh?

ANSWER # 53

The capital of Ecuador is Quito. Ecuador is located in Western South America, bordering on the Pacific Ocean at the Equator between Columbia and Peru. Ecuador is bordered by Columbia on the north; Peru on the south and the Pacific Ocean on the west.

ANSWER # 54

The capital of Miramar is Rangoon. Miramar (once Burma) is border by China on the northeast, Thailand on the southeast, India on the northwest, Laos on the east, Bangladesh on the west, the Bay of Bengal on the southwest and the Andaman Sea on the south.

QUESTION # 55

What is the capital of Morocco? Is it a) Porto-Novo b) Rabat or c) Malabo?

QUESTION # 56

What is the capital of Armenia? Is it a) Ankara b) Beirut or c) Yerevan?

ANSWER # 55

The capital of Morocco is Rabat. Northern African Morocco borders Algeria to the east, and Western Sahara to the south where its borders Mauritania. Morocco has a coast on the Atlantic Ocean that reaches past the Strait of Gibraltar to the Mediterranean Sea.

ANSWER # 56

The capital of Armenia is Yerevan. Armenia, which is officially known as the Republic of Armenia, is a mountainous country is located in the Caucasus region. The four countries that border Armenia are Iran, Azerbaijan, Georgia and Turkey.

QUESTION # 57

What is the capital of Belgium? Is it a) Brussels b) Amsterdam or c) Vaduz?

QUESTION # 58

What is the capital of Antigua and Barbuda? Is it a) Port-of-Spain b) Saint John's or c) Nassau?

ANSWER # 57

The capital of Belgium is Brussels. While bordering on the North Sea, Belgium shares borders with France, Luxembourg, and the Netherlands (Holland). Belgium comprised of the following regions: Flanders; Wallonia and Brussels.

ANSWER # 58

The capital of Antigua and Barbuda is Saint John's. Antigua and Barbuda is an island nation; hence it does not share any land border with any other nation. It is located near Montserrat (UK), Anguilla (UK), Saint Kitts and Nevis, and Guadeloupe (France).

QUESTION # 59

What is the capital of Togo? Is it a) Brazzaville b) Kinshasa or c) Lome?

QUESTION # 60

What is the difference between the Balkans and the Baltic States?

ANSWER # 59

The capital of Togo is Lome. Togo is is bordered by Ghana to the west; Benin to the east and Burkina Faso to the north. Togo extends south to the Gulf of Guinea. This Western African country is long and narrow with an interior plateau rising to mountains in the north.

ANSWER # 60

The Baltic States all border on the Baltic Sea and are found in Northern Europe (Sweden, Finland, Estonia, etc.). The Balkans, which is found in Southern Europe, refers to the countries that evolved out of former Yugoslavia (Croatia, Serbia, etc.).

QUESTION # 61

What is the capital of Taiwan? Is it a) Taipei b) Naha or c) Seoul?

QUESTION # 62

What is the capital of the Czech Republic? Is it a) Budapest b) Prague or c) Warsaw?

ANSWER # 61

The capital of Taiwan is Taipei. Located in the western Pacific Ocean, Taiwan is bordered by the Philippine Sea in the east; by the Luzon Strait on the south; and by the East China Sea to the north. Its former name "Formosa" came from Portuguese sailors – "Beautiful Island".

ANSWER # 62

The capital of the Czech Republic is Prague. The Czech Republic is bordered by Germany to the west; Austria to the south; Slovenia to the east and Poland to the north. Almost entirely surrounded by mountains, mountains mark a natural boundary with Germany and Poland.

QUESTION # 63

What is the capital of Sri Lanka? Is it a) New Delhi b) Rangoon or c) Colombo?

QUESTION # 64

What is the capital of Tonga? Is it a) Nuku'alofa b) Majuro or c) Honiara?

ANSWER # 63

The capital of Sri Lanka is Colombo. Sri Lanka is an island nation and, therefore, has maritime borders with India and the Maldives (island nation in Indian Ocean). However, it does share a tiny land border (50 yards) with India on one of its smaller islands between the two countries.

ANSWER # 64

The capital of Tonga is Nuku'alofa. Tonga is a sovereign state and an archipelago of 176 islands scattered over 270,000 sq. miles of the South Pacific Ocean. Fifty-two of these islands are inhabited. It lies 1/3 the distance between New Zealand and Hawaii.

QUESTION # 65

What is the capital of Syria? Is it a) Amman b) Damascus or c) Beirut?

QUESTION # 66

What is the capital of Switzerland? Is it a) Vienna b) Budapest or c) Bern?

ANSWER # 65

The capital of Syria is Damascus. Syria is bordered by Turkey on the north; Lebanon and Israel on the west; Iraq on the east and Jordan on the south. It consists of mountain ranges in the west and further inland a steppe area. The Syrian Desert is in the east.

ANSWER # 66

The capital of Switzerland is Bern. Switzerland is bordered by Germany to the north; France to the west; Austria and Liechtenstein to the east; and Italy to the south. The federal state of Switzerland consists of 26 cantons or member states.

QUESTION # 67

What is the capital of Trinidad and Tobago? Is it a) Port-of-Spain b) Bridgetown or c) Georgetown?

QUESTION # 68

What is the capital of Swaziland? Is it a) Maseru b) Mbabane or c) Harare?

ANSWER # 67

> The capital of Trinidad and Tobago is Port-of-Spain. These two main islands composed of nine regions are located in the northern edge of South America, lying just off the northeastern coast of Venezuela and south of Grenada in the Lesser Antilles.

ANSWER # 68

> The capital of Swaziland is Mbabane. Swaziland is bordered on the north, west and southwest by South Africa and on the east by Mozambique. This small, landlocked nation, consisting mostly of high plateaus and mountains is governed by an absolute constitutional monarchy.

QUESTION # 69

What is the capital of Tajikistan? Is it a) Bishkek b) Astana or c) Dushanbe?

QUESTION # 70

What is the capital of Cyprus? Is it a) Nicosia b) Belgrade or c) Zagreb?

ANSWER # 69

> The capital of Tajikistan is Dushanbe. This country borders Afghanistan to the south; Uzbekistan to the west; Kyrgyzstan to the north and China to the east. This landlocked Central Asian country is made up mostly of a population that is a Persian-speaking Tajik ethnic group.

ANSWER # 70

> The capital of Cyprus is Nicosia. Cyprus is the third largest and third most populous island in the Mediterranean Sea. It is located east of Greece, south of Turkey, west of Syria and Lebanon, northwest of Israel and the Gaza Strip and north of Egypt.

QUESTION # 71

What is the capital of Yemen? Is it a) Riyadh b) Sana'a or c) Doha?

QUESTION # 72

What is the capital of Zimbabwe? Is it a) Luanda b) Harare or c) Niamey?

ANSWER # 71

The capital of Yemen is Sana'a. Yemen is located in Western Asia, occupying the southern end of the Arabian Peninsula. It is bordered by Saudi Arabia to the north; the Red Sea to the west; the Gulf of Aden and the Arabian Sea to the south and Oman to the east.

ANSWER # 72

The capital of Zimbabwe is Niamey. Zimbabwe is bordered on the north by Zambia; on the northeast and east by Mozambique; on the south by South Africa; and on the southwest and west by Botswana. Landlocked, it lies between the Zambezi and Limpopo rivers.

QUESTION # 73

What is the capital of Vietnam? Is it a) Vientiane b) Hanoi or c) Phnom-Penh?

QUESTION # 74

What is the capital of Portugal? Is it a) Cadiz b) Seville or c) Lisbon?

ANSWER # 73

The capital of Vietnam is Hanoi. This S-shaped country, which lies on the eastern margin of the Indochinese Peninsula, borders the Gulf of Thailand, Gulf of Tonkin, and South China Sea, alongside China, Laos and Cambodia.

ANSWER # 74

The capital of Portugal is Lisbon. The Portuguese Republic is the westernmost country in Europe. It is situated on the Iberian Peninsula with Spain. Portugal is bordered by Spain on the east and the north and by the Atlantic Ocean on the west and the south.

QUESTION # 75

What is the difference between an atoll and an archipelago?

QUESTION # 76

What is the capital of Canada? Is it a) Montreal b) Toronto or c) Ottawa?

ANSWER # 75

> An atoll is a ring-shaped coral reef including a coral rim that encircles a lagoon partially or completely. In short, atolls are islands of coral. Archipelagos are clusters of islands that share a common origin, often volcanic.

ANSWER # 76

> The capital of Canada is Ottawa. Canada is an example of a non-island country that shares its borders with one country only, in this case the United States. Other such states are San Marino, Portugal, Denmark, South Korea, Gambia and the Vatican City, amongst others.

QUESTION # 77

What is the capital of Argentina? Is it a) Bogota b) Caracas or c) Buenos Aires?

QUESTION # 78

What is the capital of Qatar? Is it a) Bagdad b) Doha or c) Tehran?

ANSWER # 77

The capital of Argentina is Buenos Aires. Argentina is bordered by Chile to the west and south; Bolivia and Paraguay to the north and Brazil and Uruguay to the northeast. Argentina is a plain, rising from the Atlantic Ocean to the Chilean border and the Andes Mountain peaks.

ANSWER # 78

The capital of Qatar is Doha. Qatar is a sovereign state located in Western Asia, occupying the small Qatar Peninsula in the much larger Arabian Peninsula. Its sole land border is with Saudi Arabia to the south with the rest of its territory surrounded by the Persian Gulf.

QUESTION # 79

What is the capital of Poland? Is it a) Budapest b) Vienna or c) Warsaw?

QUESTION # 80

What is the capital of Philippines? Is it a) Manila b) Apia or c) Naha?

ANSWER # 79

The capital of Poland is Warsaw. Poland is bordered by Germany to the west; the Czech Republic and Slovakia to the south; Ukraine and Belarus to the east and Lithuania and the Russian province of Kaliningrad Oblast to the northeast. The Baltic Sea is on the north.

ANSWER # 80

The capital of Philippines is Manila. The Philippines is an archipelago of 7,107 islands bordered by the Philippine Sea to the east; the South China Sea to the west and the Celebes Sea to the south. The island of Borneo is located to the southwest and Taiwan is directly north.

QUESTION # 81

What is the capital of Senegal? Is it a) Bangui b) Dakar or c) Windhoek?

QUESTION # 82

What is the capital of Saudi Arabia? Is it a) Sana'a b) Doha or c) Riyadh?

ANSWER # 81

The capital of Senegal is Dakar. This West African country owes its name to the Senegal River that is located to its east and north. Senegal is bordered by the Atlantic Ocean to the west; Mali to the east; Mauritania to the north and Guinea and Guinea-Bissau to the south.

ANSWER # 82

The capital of Saudi Arabia is Riyadh. It is bordered by Jordan and Iraq to the north; Kuwait to the northeast; Qatar, Bahrain and the United Arab Emirates to the east; Yemen to the south; Oman to the southeast; the Red Sea to the west and the Persian Gulf to the east.

QUESTION # 83

What is the capital of Nepal? Is it a) Kathmandu b) Kabul or c) Islamabad?

QUESTION # 84

What is the capital of Samoa? Is it a) Port Moresby b) Apia or c) Naha?

ANSWER # 83

The capital of Nepal is Kathmandu. Nepal is located in the Himalayas and bordered to the north by the People' Republic of China and the south, east and west by the Republic of India. Northern Nepal has 8 out of 10 of the world's tallest mountains (the tallest – Mount Everest).

ANSWER # 84

The capital of Samoa is Apia. It is located south of the Equator, about halfway between Hawaii and New Zealand in the Polynesian region of the Pacific. It has two large islands named Upolu and Savaii which account for 99% of its land area, and eight small islets.

QUESTION # 85

What is the capital of Rwanda? Is it a) Asmara b) Lilongwe or c) Kigali?

0
QUESTION # 86

What is the capital of Seychelles? Is it a) Victoria b) Lusaka or c) Antananarivo?

ANSWER # 85

The capital of Rwanda is Kigali. This central and east African country (a few degrees south of the Equator) is bordered by Uganda, Tanzania, Burundi and the Democratic Republic of the Congo. At high elevation, it has mountains in the west, a savanna in the east, and "lakes".

ANSWER # 86

The capital of Seychelles is Victoria. Seychelles is 115-island spanning an archipelago in the Indian Ocean east of mainland Africa. It is northeast of the island of Madagascar; Zanzibar to the west; Mauritius to the south and Comoros and Mayotte to the southwest.

QUESTION # 87

What is the capital of Solomon Islands?
Is it a) Apia b) Honiara or c) Majuro?

QUESTION # 88

What is the capital of Denmark? Is it a) Helsinki b) Vilnius or c) Copenhagen?

ANSWER # 87

> The capital of the Solomon Islands is Honiara. The Solomon Islands are a sovereign country consisting of large number of islands in Oceania lying to the east of Padua New Guinea and lying northwest of Vanuatu. Its capital, Honiara, is on the island of Guadalcanal.

ANSWER # 88

> The capital of Denmark is Copenhagen. In the Scandinavian region of Northern Europe, Denmark is southwest of Sweden, south of Norway and bordered to the south by Germany. Demark consists of a peninsula, Jutland, and the Danish archipelago of 407 islands.

QUESTION # 89

What is the capital of Cambodia? Is it a) Phnom-Penh b) Vientiane or c) Rangoon?

QUESTION # 90

What is the difference between a rainforest and tundra?

ANSWER # 89

The capital of Cambodia is Phnom-Penh. Cambodia (once the Khmer Empire) is located in the southern portion of Indochina Peninsula. It is bordered by Thailand to the northwest; Laos to the northeast; Vietnam to the east and the Gulf of Thailand to the southwest.

ANSWER # 90

A rainforest is a hot, thick jungle that gets a lot of rain and is located around the middle of the earth near the equator. Exports include chocolate, sugar and medicine. Tundra is a vast, flat, treeless Arctic region in which the subsoil is permanently frozen.

QUESTION # 91

What is the capital of Benin? Is it a) Accra b) Porto-Novo or c) Manama?

QUESTION # 92

What is the capital of South Africa? Is it a) Pretoria b) Cape town or c) Bloemfontein?

ANSWER # 91

> The capital of Benin is Porto-Novo. Benin. Benin is bordered by Togo to the west; by Nigeria to the east and by Burkina Faso and Niger to the north. The majority of the populations live on its small southern coastline on the Bight of Benin. [Seat of government is Cottonou].

ANSWER # 92

> The capitals of South Africa are Pretoria (executive), Capetown (legislative) and Bloemfontein (Judicial). It is bordered to the north by Namibia, Botswana and Zimbabwe; to Swaziland and Mozambique to the east while Lesotho is an enclave surrounded by it.

QUESTION # 93

What is the capital of Albania? Is it a) Tirana b) Sofia or c) Belgrade?

QUESTION # 94

What is the capital of Finland? Is it a) Riga b) Helsinki or c) Tallinn?

ANSWER # 93

The capital of Albania is Tirana. Albania is bordered by Montenegro to the northwest; Kosovo (disputed) to the northeast; Macedonia to the east; and Greece to the south and southeast. It has a coast on the Adriatic Sea to the west and on the Ionian Sea to the southeast.

ANSWER # 94

The capital of Finland is Helsinki. Finland is a Nordic country in the Fennoscandian region of Northern Europe. It is bordered by Sweden to the west; Norway to the north and Russia to the east while Estonia lies to the south across the Bay of Finland.

QUESTION # 95

What is the capital of Bangladesh? Is it a) Islamabad b) Kabul or c) Dhaka?

QUESTION # 96

What is the capital of Eritrea? Is it a) Asmara b) Khartoum or c) Mogadishu?

ANSWER # 95

The capital of Bangladesh is Dhaka. Bangladesh is bordered by India and Burma to the north, west and east. It is separated from Nepal, Bhutan and China by India's narrow Siliguri Corridor. It straddles the fertile basis of 3 Asian rivers: the Ganges, the Jamuna and Meghna.

ANSWER # 96

The capital of Eritrea is Asmara. Eritrea is bordered by Sudan in the west; Ethiopia in the south and Djibouti in the southeast. The northeastern and eastern parts of Eritrea have an extensive coastline along the Red Sea, directly across from Saudi Arabia and Yemen.

QUESTION # 97

What is the capital of Bahrain? Is it a) Baku b) Manama or c) Minsk?

QUESTION # 98

What is the capital of Bhutan? Is it a) Dhaka b) Islamabad or c) Thimphu?

ANSWER # 97

The capital of Bahrain is Manama. Bahrain is a small island country situated near the western shores of the Persian Gulf. It is an archipelago of 33 islands, the largest being Bahrain Island (34 miles long and 11 miles wide). Saudi Arabia (to the west;) is connected by a causeway.

ANSWER # 98

The capital of Bhutan is Thimphu. This landlocked state is at the end of the Himalayas. It is bordered to the north by China and to the south, east and west by the Republic of India. Further west, it is separated from Nepal by the Indian state of Sikkim and Bangladesh by Assam.

QUESTION # 99

What is the capital of Cuba? Is it a) Havana b) Kingston or c) Saint John's?

QUESTION # 100

What is the capital of Botswana? Is it a) Kampala b) Gaborone or c) Maputo?

ANSWER # 99

The capital of Cuba is Havana. This island country in the Caribbean has maritime borders with the United States to the north; the Bahamas and Mexico to the west; the Cayman Islands and Jamaica to the south Haiti and the Dominican Republic and to the south.

ANSWER # 100

The capital of Botswana is Gaborone. This landlocked country is bordered by South Africa to the south and southeast; Namibia to the west and north and Zimbabwe to the northeast. Botswana is flat and up to 70% is covered by the Kalahari Desert.

QUESTION # 101

What is the capital of Bosnia and Herzegovina? Is it a) Belgrade b) Zagreb or c) Sarajevo?

QUESTION # 102

What is the capital of Fiji? Is it a) Suva b) Apia or c) Honiara?

ANSWER # 101

The capital of Bosnia and Herzegovina is Sarajevo. Bosnia is (on the Balkan Peninsula) bordered by Croatia to the north, west and south; Serbia to the east and Montenegro to the southeast. Bosnia is almost landlocked except for the 12 miles of coastline on the Adriatic Sea.

ANSWER # 102

The capital of Fiji is Suva. Fiji is an island country in Melanesia in the South Pacific Ocean about 1,100 nautical miles northeast of New Zealand. Its closest neighbors are Vanuatu to the west; France's New Caledonia to the southwest and Tonga to the east and Tuvalu (north).

QUESTION # 103

What is the capital of Georgia? Is it a) Baku b) Tbilisi or c) Yerevan?

QUESTION # 104

What is the capital of Brunei? Is it a) Thimphu b) Doha or c) Bandar Seri Begawan?

ANSWER # 103

> The capital of Georgia is Tbilisi. Georgia is bordered to the west by the Black Sea; to the north by Russia; to the south by Turkey and Armenia and to the southeast by Azerbaijan. It is in the Caucus region of Eurasia at the crossroads of Western Asia and Eastern Europe.

ANSWER # 104

> The capital of Brunei is Bandar Seri Begawan. Brunei is a sovereign state located on the north coast of Borneo in Southeast Asia. Apart from its coastline with the South China Sea, it is completely surrounded by the state of Sarawak, Malaysia (it is completely on Borneo).

QUESTION # 105

What is the difference between latitude and longitude?

QUESTION # 106

What is the capital of Burundi? Is it a) Bujumbura b) Dakar or c) Kigali?

ANSWER # 105

Latitude specifies a location's distance north or south of the Equator. Longitude specifies a location's distance east or west from an imaginary line connecting the North and South Poles, called the Prime Meridian. Latitudes are called parallels and longitudes are called meridians.

ANSWER # 106

The capital of Burundi is Bujumbura. Bujumbura, its main port, is located on the northeastern shore of Lake Tanganyika. Burundi is bordered on the north by Rwanda, by Tanzania on the east and south, and on the west by the Democratic Republic of the Congo.

QUESTION # 107

What is the capital of Cape Verde? Is it a) Windhoek b) Praia or c) Moroni?

QUESTION # 108

What is the capital of Cameroon? Is it a) Dar es Salaam b) Gaborone or c) Yaoundé?

ANSWER # 107

The capital of Cape Verde is Praia. Cape Verde is an island country spanning an archipelago of 10 islands located in the central Atlantic Ocean 350 miles off the coast of Western Africa. The islands, covering an area of slightly over 15,000 sq. mi., are of volcanic origin.

ANSWER # 108

The capital of Cameroon is Yaoundé. Cameroon is a country in the west Central Africa region bordered by Nigeria to the west, Chad to the northeast, the Central African Republic to the east and Equatorial Guinea, Gabon and the Republic of the Congo to the south.

QUESTION # 109

What is the capital of Central African Republic? Is it a) Bangui b) Abuja or c) Libreville?

QUESTION # 110

What is the capital of Peru? Is it a) Santiago b) Lima or c) Buenos Aires?

ANSWER # 109

The capital of Central African Republic is Bangui. This landlocked country in Central Africa borders Chad in the north; Sudan in the northeast; South Sudan in the east; the Democratic Republic of the Congo, the Republic of the Congo in the south and Cameroon in the west.

ANSWER # 110

The capital of Peru is Lima. Peru, which is located in western South America, is bordered in the north by Ecuador and Columbia; in the east by Brazil; in the southeast by Bolivia; in the south by Chile and in the west by the Pacific Ocean. Peru was once home to the Incas.

QUESTION # 111

What is the capital of Tanzania? Is it a) Monrovia b) Libreville or c) Dar es Salaam?

QUESTION # 112

What is the capital of Laos? Is it a) Vientiane b) Phnom-Penh or c) Rangoon?

ANSWER # 111

The capital of Tanzania is Dar es Salaam. Tanzania is a country in East Africa which is bordered by Kenya and Uganda to the north; Rwanda, Burundi and the Democratic Republic of the Congo to the west and Zambia, Malawi and Mozambique to the south.

ANSWER # 112

The capital of Laos is Vientiane. Laos is a landlocked country in Southeast Asia that is bordered by Burma and China to the northwest; Vietnam to the east; Cambodia to the south and Thailand to the west. Its thickly forested landscape consists mostly of rugged mountains.

QUESTION # 113

What is the capital of Kyrgyzstan? Is it a) Tbilisi b) Bishkek or c) Baku?

QUESTION # 114

What is the capital of North Korea? Is it a) Naha b) Taipei or c) Pyongyang?

ANSWER # 113

The capital of Kyrgyzstan is Bishkek. Kyrgyzstan is a country located in Central Asia that is bordered by Kazakhstan to the north; Uzbekistan to the west; Tajikistan to the southeast and China to the east. The mountainous region of Tian Shan covers 80% of the country.

ANSWER # 114

The capital of North Korea is Pyongyang. North Korea is a country in East Asia, in the northern half of the Korean Peninsula. The Yalu (Amnok) River and the Tumen River [a section separates North Korea from Russia] form the international border between North Korea and China.

QUESTION # 115

What is the capital of Lebanon? Is it a) Beirut b) Amman or c) Damascus?

QUESTION # 116

What is the capital of Burkina? Is it a) Sofia b) Ouagadougou or c) Belgrade?

ANSWER # 115

The capital of Lebanon is Beirut. Lebanon is a country in the East Mediterranean bordered by Syria to the north and east and Israel to the south. Its location is at the crossroads of the Mediterranean Basin and the Arabian hinterlands (land beyond a coast).

ANSWER # 116

The capital of Burkina Faso is Ouagadougou. Burkina (short name) is a landlocked country in west Africa bordered by Mali to the north; Niger to the east; Benin to the southeast; Togo and Ghana to the south and the Ivory Coast to the southwest.

QUESTION # 117

What is the capital of Thailand? Is it a) Rangoon b) Phnom-Penh or c) Bangkok?

QUESTION # 118

What is the capital of Chile? Is it a) Santiago b) Lima or c) Buenos Aires?

ANSWER # 117

The capital of Thailand is Bangkok. Thailand (formerly Siam) is bordered to the north by Burma and Laos; to the east by Laos and Cambodia; to the south by the Gulf of Thailand and Malaysia and to the west by the Andaman Sea and the southern extremity of Burma.

ANSWER # 118

The capital of Chile is Santiago. Chile occupies a long strip of land between the Andes Mountains and the Pacific Ocean. It is bordered by Peru to the north; Bolivia to the northeast; Argentina to the east and the Drake Passage to the south. Chilean territory includes Easter Island.

QUESTION # 119

What is the capital of Kazakhstan? Is it a) Tashkent b) Astana or c) Tbilisi?

QUESTION # 120

Why isn't the oceanic island of New Zealand (which is located near Australia) not considered to be a continent?

ANSWER # 119

> The capital of Kazakhstan is Astana. Kazakhstan is the world's largest landlocked country. It is neighbored clockwise from the north by Russia, China, Kyrgyzstan, Uzbekistan, and Turkmenistan. It also borders on a large part of the Caspian Sea.

ANSWER # 120

> New Zealand is not one of the seven continents (Europe, Australia, Africa, Antarctica, North America, Asia, and South America). It is, therefore, considered a part of a region of the world. In this case, it is considered to be a part of the "Australia and Oceanic" region.

QUESTION # 121

What is the capital of Macedonia? Is it a) Bucharest b) Skopje or c) Zagreb?

QUESTION # 122

What is the capital of the United Arab Emirate? Is it a) Abu Dhabi b) Doha or c) Addis Ababa?

ANSWER # 121

> The capital of Macedonia is Skopje. Macedonia, one of the successor states to Yugoslavia, is a landlocked country in the central Balkan Peninsula. It is bordered by Kosovo to the northwest; Serbia to the north; Bulgaria to the east; Greece to the south and Albania to the west.

ANSWER # 122

> The capital of the United Arab Emirates is Abu Dhabi. The United Arab Emirates are an Arab country in the southeast of the Arabian Peninsula on the Persian Gulf, bordering Oman to the east and Saudi Arabia to the south, as well as sharing sea borders with Qatar and Iran.

QUESTION # 123

What is the capital of Turkmenistan? Is it a) Dushanbe b) Ashgabat or c) Baku?

QUESTION # 124

What is the capital of Oman? Is it a) Sana'a b) Doha or c) Muscat?

ANSWER #123

The capital of Turkmenistan is Ashgabat. Turkmenistan (a Turkic state in Central Asia) is bordered by Afghanistan to the southeast; Iran to the south and southwest; Uzbekistan to the east and northeast; Kazakhstan to the northwest and the Caspian Sea to the west.

ANSWER # 124

The capital of Oman is Muscat. Oman is bordered by the United Arab Emirates to the northwest; Saudi Arabia to the west; Yemen to the southeast and it shares a maritime border with Iran. The coast is formed by the Arabian Sea (southeast) and the Gulf of Oman (northeast).

QUESTION # 125

What is the capital of Mongolia? Is it a) Ulan Bator b) Kiev or c) Vilnius?

QUESTION # 126

What is the capital of Dominican Republic? Is it a) San Jose b) Santa Domingo or c) Managua?

ANSWER # 125

> The capital of Mongolia is Ulan Bator. Mongolia is a landlocked country in East and Central Asia that borders Russia to the north and the Inner Mongolia region of China to the south, east and west. About 45% of the population lives in the capital and largest city, Ulan Bator.

ANSWER # 126

> The capital of the Dominican Republic is Santa Domingo. Santa Dominican shares the island of Hispaniola (Greater Antilles archipelago) with Haiti, which is on the western third of the island. Saint Martin is the only other island that has the same arrangement, sharing with two nations.

QUESTION # 127

What is the capital of East Timor? Is it a) Jakarta b) Kuala Lumpur or c) Dili?

QUESTION # 128

What is the capital of Iran? Is it a) Tehran b) Bagdad or c) Amman?

ANSWER # 127

The capital of East Timor is Dili. East Timor is a country in Southeast Asia that comprises the eastern part of the island of Timor, the nearby islands o Atauro and Jaco and Oecusse, an enclave on the northwestern side of the island, within Indonesian West Timor.

ANSWER # 128

The capital of Iran is Tehran. Iran is a country in Western Asia. It is bordered on the north by Armenia, Azerbaijan and Turkmenistan; on the east by Afghanistan and Pakistan; on the south by the Persian Gulf and the Gulf of Oman; on the west by Iraq and on the northwest by Turkey.

QUESTION # 129

What is the capital of Malawi? Is it a) Nouakchott b) Lilongwe or c) Brazzaville?

QUESTION # 130

What is the capital of Ethiopia? Is it a) Tripoli b) Asmara or c) Addis Ababa?

ANSWER # 129

The capital of Malawi is Lilongwe. The southeastern African country of Malawi occupies a thin strip of land between Zambia and Mozambique. In the north and northeast, it also shares a border with Tanzania. Landlocked, it is connected to the Mozambique ports, Nacala and Beira.

ANSWER # 130

The capital of Ethiopia is Addis Ababa. Ethiopia, which is located in the Horn of Africa, (easternmost part of the African landmass) is a country that is bordered by Eritrea to the north; Djibouti and Somalia to the east; Sudan and South Sudan to the west; and Kenya to the south.

QUESTION # 131

What is the capital of Mauritius? Is it a) Port Louis b) Muscat or c) Dili?

QUESTION # 132

What is the capital of Palau? Is it a) Manila b) Melekeok or c) Jakarta?

ANSWER # 131

> The capital of Mauritius is Port Louis. Mauritius is an island nation in the Indian Ocean about 1, 200 miles off the southeast coast of the African continent. The country includes the islands of Mauritius, Rodrigues and the islands of Agalega and Saint Brandon.

ANSWER # 132

> The capital of Palau is Melekeok. Palau is an island country in the western Pacific Ocean. Geographically, it is part of the larger island group of Micronesia. Its population is about 21,000 people, spread out over the 250 islands that form the west chain of the Caroline Islands.

QUESTION # 133

What is the capital of Estonia? Is it a) Riga b) Vilnius or c) Tallinn?

QUESTION # 134

What is the capital of Moldova? Is it a) Chisinau b) Bucharest or c) Budapest?

ANSWER # 133

The capital of Estonia is Tallinn. Estonia is in the Baltic region. It is bordered to the north by the Gulf of Finland; to the west by the Baltic Sea; to the south by Latvia and to the east by Lake Peipus and Russia. Across the Baltic Sea lies Sweden to the west and Finland to the north.

ANSWER # 134

The capital of Moldova is Chisinau. Moldova lies between Romania to the west and Ukraine to the north. Most of its land lies between two rivers, the Dniester and the Prut. The western border is formed by the Prut River, joins the Danube River, then the Black Sea.

QUESTION # 135

What are the Arctic Circle and the Antarctic Circles?

QUESTION # 136

What is the capital of Israel? Is it a) Tel Aviv b) Jerusalem or c) Haifa?

ANSWER # 135

The Arctic Circle is one of the five major circles of latitude that mark maps of the Earth. It is a parallel of latitude that runs 66 degrees 33 ' 39 minutes (as of the year 2000) north of the Equator. The equivalent latitude in the southern hemisphere is called the Antarctic Circle.

ANSWER # 136

The capital of Israel is Jerusalem. After the State of Israel was founded in 1948, it recognized Jerusalem as its capital in 1950. Today, their parliament, the Knesset, is located in Jerusalem while most countries maintain their embassies in Tel Aviv due to the Palastine question.

QUESTION # 137

What is the capital of The Gambia? Is it a) Abuja b) Accra or c) Banjul?

QUESTION # 138

What is the capital of Iraq? Is it a) Bagdad b) Tehran or c) Ankara?

ANSWER # 137

> The capital of The Gambia is Banjul. The Gambia is a country in West Africa that is surrounded by Senegal, apart from a short strip of Atlantic coastline at its western end. It is a very small and narrow country whose borders mirror the meanderings of the Gambia River.

ANSWER # 138

> The capital of Iraq is Bagdad. Iraq is a country in Western Asia that borders Syria to the northwest; Turkey to the north; Iran to the east; Jordan to the west; Saudi Arabia to the south and southwest and Kuwait to the south. Iraq has a narrow section of coastline on the Persian Gulf.

QUESTION # 139

What is the capital of Uzbekistan? Is it a) Tbilisi b) Tashkent or c) Baku?

QUESTION # 140

What is the capital of Equatorial Guinea? Is it a) Niamey b) Bamako or c) Malabo?

ANSWER # 139

The capital of Uzbekistan is Tashkent. Uzbekistan is a Central Asian country that borders Kazakhstan to the west and to the north; Kyrgyzstan and Tajikistan to the east and Afghanistan and Turkmenistan to the south. It is one of two (doubly landlocked worldwide).

ANSWER # 140

The capital of Equatorial Guinea is Malabo. One of the smallest countries in Middle Africa, it has 2 regions: insular and mainland. Its 2 islands are Bioko and Annabon Islands. The main region is bordered by Cameroon on the north and Gabon on the south and east.

QUESTION # 141

What is the capital of Ivory Coast? Is it a) Yamoussoukro b) Porto-Novo or c) Niamey?

QUESTION # 142

What is the capital of Comoros? Is it a) Kinshasa b) Moroni or c) Mogadishu?

ANSWER # 141

The capital of Ivory Coast (Cote D'Ivoire) is Yamoussoukro. The Ivory Coast is a country in West Africa that borders Liberia and Guinea in the west; Mali and Burkina Faso in the north; Ghana in the east and the Gulf of Guinea (Atlantic Ocean) in the south.

ANSWER # 142

The capital of Comoros is Moroni. Comoros is an archipelago island nation in the Indian Ocean, located in the northern end of the Mozambique Channel off the eastern coast of Africa between northeastern Mozambique and northwestern Madagascar.

QUESTION # 143

What is the capital of Liechtenstein? Is it a) Amsterdam b) Brussels or c) Vaduz?

QUESTION # 144

What is the capital of Democratic Republic of the Congo? Is it a) Brazzaville b) Kinshasa or c) Mogadishu?

ANSWER # 143

The capital of Liechtenstein is Vaduz. Liechtenstein is a doubly landlocked country in Central Europe. [The other doubly landlocked country in the world is Uzbekistan]. It is bordered by Switzerland to the west and south and by Austria to the east and north.

ANSWER # 144

The capital of the Democratic Republic of the Congo is Brazzaville. This country borders the Central African Republic and South Sudan (north); Uganda, Rwanda and Burundi (east); Zambia and Angola (west) and the Republic of Congo and Atlantic Ocean (west).

QUESTION # 145

What is the capital of Ghana? Is it a) Dakar b) Accra or c) Mobako?

QUESTION # 146

What is the capital of Kiribati? Is it a) Apia b) Honiara or c) Tarawa Atoll?

ANSWER # 145

The capital of Ghana is Accra. Ghana is a West African country that is bordered by the Ivory Coast (Cote d'Ivoire) to the west; Burkina Faso to the north; Togo to the east and the Gulf of Guinea to the south. Ghana is just north of the Equator; the Prime Meridian through it.

ANSWER # 146

The capital of Kiribati is Tarawa Atoll. Kiribati is an island nation located in the central tropical Pacific Ocean. The island nation is composed of 32 atolls and one raised coral island straddling the equator and bordering the International Date Line at its easternmost point.

QUESTION # 147

What is the capital of Madagascar? Is it a) Antananarivo b) Khartoum or c) Nairobi?

QUESTION # 148

What is the capital of Malta? Is it a) Tirana b) Valletta or c) Sofia?

ANSWER # 147

> The capital of Madagascar is Antananarivo. Known once as the Malagasy Republic, this island country lies in the Indian Ocean, off the southeastern coast of Africa. The fourth largest island in the world, it is joined by numerous small peripheral islands.

ANSWER # 148

> The capital of Malta is Valetta. Malta is a southern European country consisting of an archipelago situated in the center of the Mediterranean Sea east of Tunisia and north of Libya. Malta covers just over 122 sq. mi. in land mass, making it one of the smallest states.

QUESTION # 149

What is the capital of Marshall Islands?
Is it a) Honiara b) Apia or c) Majuro?

QUESTION # 150

While neither Cape is at the most southerly tip of their respective continents (a misconception that once existed until finally surveyed), under which continents are the Cape of Good Hope and Cape Horn located?

ANSWER # 149

The capital of the Marshall Islands is Majuro. Marshall Islands is an island country located in the northern Pacific Ocean. This country is part of the larger island group of Micronesia, with people spread out over 34 low-lying coral atolls, comprising 1,156 islands and islets.

ANSWER # 150

The Cape of Good Hope is a rocky headland on the Atlantic coast of the Cape Peninsula, South Africa. [The southernmost point is Cape Agulhas]. Cape Horn (below South America) is a "sailor's graveyard" due to strong winds, large waves, strong currents and icebergs.

Index of Countries/Capitals

A

Afghanistan (Kabul) p. 8
Albania (Tirana) p. 98
Antigua & Barbuda (Saint John's) p. 64
Armenia (Yerevan) p. 60
Argentina (Buenos Aires) p. 82
Australia (Canberra) p. 14
Azerbaijan (Baku) p. 52

B

The Bahamas (Nassau) p. 32
Bahrain (Manama) p. 102
Bangladesh (Dhaka) p. 100
Barbados (Bridgetown) p. 16
Belarus (Minsk) p. 56
Belize (Belmopan) p. 30
Belgium (Brussels) p. 64
Benin (Porto-Novo) p. 96
Bhutan (Thimphu) p. 102
Bolivia (La Paz; Sucre) p. 6
Bosnia & Herzegovina (Sarajevo) p. 106
Botswana (Gaborone) p. 104
Brunei (Bandar Seri Begawan) p. 108
Bulgaria (Sofia) p. 26
Burkina Faso (Ouagadougou) p. 120
Burundi (Bujumbura) p. 110

C

Cambodia (Phnom-Penh) p. 94
Cameroon (Yaoundé) p. 112
Canada (Ottawa) p. 80
Cape Verde (Praia) p. 112

Central African Republic (Bangui) p. 114
Chad (N'Djamena) p. 42
Chile (Santiago) p. 122
Columbia (Bogota) p. 18
Comoros (Moroni) p. 146
Costa Rica (San Jose) p. 38
Croatia (Zagreb) p. 40
Cuba (Havana) p. 104
Cyprus (Nicosia) p. 74
Czech Republic (Prague) p. 66

D

Democratic Republic of the Congo (Brazzaville) p. 148
Denmark (Copenhagen) p. 92
Dominican Republic (Santa Domingo) p. 130

E

East Timor (Dili) p. 132
Ecuador (Quito) p. 58
Egypt (Cairo) p. 53
Equatorial Guinea (Malabo) p. 144
Eritrea (Asmara) p. 100
Estonia (Tallinn) p. 138
Ethiopia (Addis Ababa) p. 134

F

Fiji (Suva) p. 106
Finland (Helsinki) p. 98

G

The Gambia (Banjul) p. 142
Georgia (Tbilisi) p. 108
Ghana (Accra) p. 150
Guinea (Conakry) p. 40

Guyana (Georgetown) p. 32

H

Haiti (Port-au-Prince) p. 46
Honduras (Tegucigalpa) p. 50
Hungary (Budapest) p. 8

I

Iceland (Reykjavik) p. 16
Iran (Tehran) p. 132
Iraq (Baghdad) p. 142
Israel (Jerusalem) p. 140
Indonesia (Jakarta) p. 42
Ivory Coast [Cote D'Ivoire] (Yamoussoukro) p. 146

J

Jamaica (Kingston) p. 24
Japan (Tokyo) p. 10

K

Kazakhstan (Astana) p. 124
Kiribati (Tarawa Atoll) p. 150
Kyrgyzstan (Bishkek) p. 118

L

Latvia (Riga) p. 44

Lebanon (Beirut) p. 120

Liberia (Monrovia) p. 48

Libya (Tripoli) p. 24

Liechtenstein (Vaduz) p. 148

Lithuania (Vilnius) p. 36

Laos (Vientiane) p. 116

M

Macedonia (Skopje) p. 126

Madagascar (Antananarivo) p. 152
Malawi (Lilongwe) p. 134
Malaysia (Kuala Lumpur) p. 46
Mali (Bamako) p. 52
Malta (Valetta) p. 152
Marshall Islands (Majuro) p. 152
Mauritius (Port Louis) p. 136
Miramar (Rangoon) p. 58
Moldova (Chisinau) p. 138
Mongolia (Ulan Bator) p. 130
Morocco (Yerevan) p. 60

N

Nepal (Kathmandu) p. 88
The Netherlands (Amsterdam) p. 26
New Zealand (Wellington) p. 10
Nicaragua (Managua) p. 28
North Korea (Pyongyang) p. 118
Norway (Oslo) p. 44

O

Oman (Muscat) p. 128

P

Palau (Melekeok) p. 136
Paraguay (Asuncion) p. 24
Peru (Lima) p. 114
Philippines (Manila) p. 84
Poland (Warsaw) p. 84
Portugal (Lisbon) p. 78
Puerto Rico (San Juan) p. 54

Q

Qatar (Doha) p. 82

R

Romania (Bucharest) p. 54

Rwanda (Kigali) p. 90

S

Samoa (Apia) p. 88
Saudi Arabia (Riyadh) p. 86
Senegal (Dakar) p. 86
Serbia (Belgrade) p. 36
Seychelles (Victoria) p. 90
Sierra Leone (Freetown) p. 34
Slovenia (Ljubljana) p. 48
Solomon Islands (Honiara) p. 92
Somalia (Mogadishu) p. 18
South Africa (Pretoria; Capetown; Bloemfontein) p. 96
Sri Lanka (Colombo) p. 68
Sudan (Khartoum) p. 6
Suriname (Paramaribo) p. 38
Swaziland (Mbabane) p. 72
Sweden (Stockholm) p. 30
Switzerland (Bern) p. 70
Syria (Damascus) p. 70

T

Taiwan (Taipei) p. 66
Tajikistan (Dushanbe) p. 74
Tanzania (Dar es Salaam) p. 116
Thailand (Bangkok) p. 122
Tonga (Nuku'alofa) p. 68
Trinidad & Tobago (Port-au-Spain) p. 72
Turkey (Ankara) p. 22
Turkmenistan (Ashgabat) p. 128

U

Uganda (Kampala) p. 12
Ukraine (Kiev) p. 14
United Arab Emirates (Abu Dhabi) p. 126

Uruguay (Montevideo) p. 12
Uzbekistan (Tashkent) p. 144

V

Vietnam (Hanoi) p. 78

Y

Yemen (Sana'a) p. 76

Z

Zambia (Lusaka) p. 28
Zimbabwe (Niamey) p. 76